HAL•LEONARD
INSTRUMENTAL PLAY-ALONG

AUDIO ACCESS INCLUDED

PLAYBACK+
Speed • Pitch • Balance • Loop

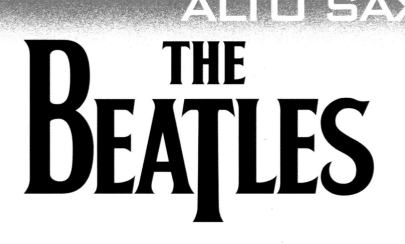
THE BEATLES

Cover Photo: Fiona Adams/Getty

To access audio visit:
www.halleonard.com/mylibrary

Enter Code
3127-0942-9739-1038

Audio Arrangements by Peter Deneff

ISBN 978-1-4950-9068-4

HAL•LEONARD®
7777 W. BLUEMOUND RD. P.O. BOX 13819 MILWAUKEE, WI 53213

In Australia Contact:
Hal Leonard Australia Pty. Ltd.
4 Lentara Court
Cheltenham, Victoria, 3192 Australia
Email: ausadmin@halleonard.com.au

Visit Hal Leonard Online at
www.halleonard.com

ALL YOU NEED IS LOVE

ALTO SAX

Words and Music by JOHN LENNON
and PAUL McCARTNEY

BLACKBIRD

ALTO SAX

Words and Music by JOHN LENNON
and PAUL McCARTNEY

DAY TRIPPER

ALTO SAX

Words and Music by JOHN LENNON
and PAUL McCARTNEY

ELEANOR RIGBY

ALTO SAX

Words and Music by JOHN LENNON
and PAUL McCARTNEY

GET BACK

ALTO SAX

Words and Music by JOHN LENNON
and PAUL McCARTNEY

HERE, THERE AND EVERYWHERE

ALTO SAX

Words and Music by JOHN LENNON
and PAUL McCARTNEY

HEY JUDE

ALTO SAX

Words and Music by JOHN LENNON
and PAUL McCARTNEY

I WILL

ALTO SAX

Words and Music by JOHN LENNON
and PAUL McCARTNEY

LET IT BE

ALTO SAX

Words and Music by JOHN LENNON
and PAUL McCARTNEY

LUCY IN THE SKY WITH DIAMONDS

ALTO SAX

Words and Music by JOHN LENNON
and PAUL McCARTNEY

OB-LA-DI, OB-LA-DA

ALTO SAX

Words and Music by JOHN LENNON
and PAUL McCARTNEY

PENNY LANE

ALTO SAX

Words and Music by JOHN LENNON
and PAUL McCARTNEY

SOMETHING

ALTO SAX

Words and Music by
GEORGE HARRISON

TICKET TO RIDE

ALTO SAX

Words and Music by JOHN LENNON
and PAUL McCARTNEY

YESTERDAY

ALTO SAX

Words and Music by JOHN LENNON
and PAUL McCARTNEY